WHY WERE CASTLES BUILT?

ANCIENT HISTORY BOOKS FOR KIDS

CHILDREN'S ANCIENT HISTORY

Castles are remarkable buildings, not very much like the houses we live in or the stores we shop at.

Why were they built that way? Let's find out!

What is a castle?

A castle is not just an impressive building. It's a special kind of structure, built for special functions.

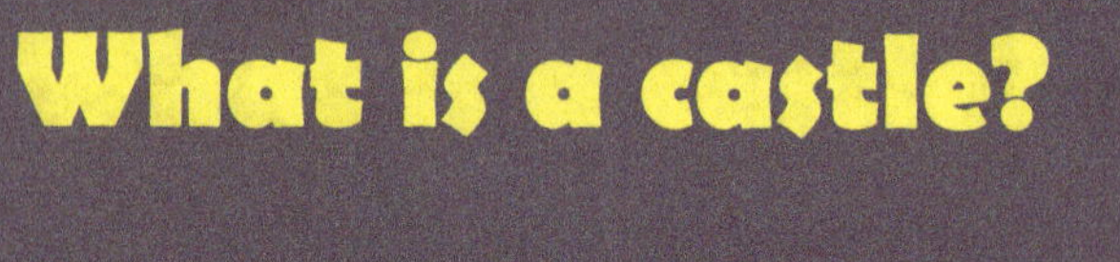

Genoese Medieval fortress

Le Mont Saint Michel

A castle is a fortified structure that was home to a noble family in Europe. This makes it different from a palace, which would be a home to a royal or noble family but was designed for comfort and show, and not for war.

Alcazar Castle

It also makes it different from a fort or a fortress, which would be designed mainly for war, with little attention to matters of comfort. Royal and noble families lived in palaces and castles in the middle ages, but rarely in their forts and fortresses except during times of war.

Alnwick Castle

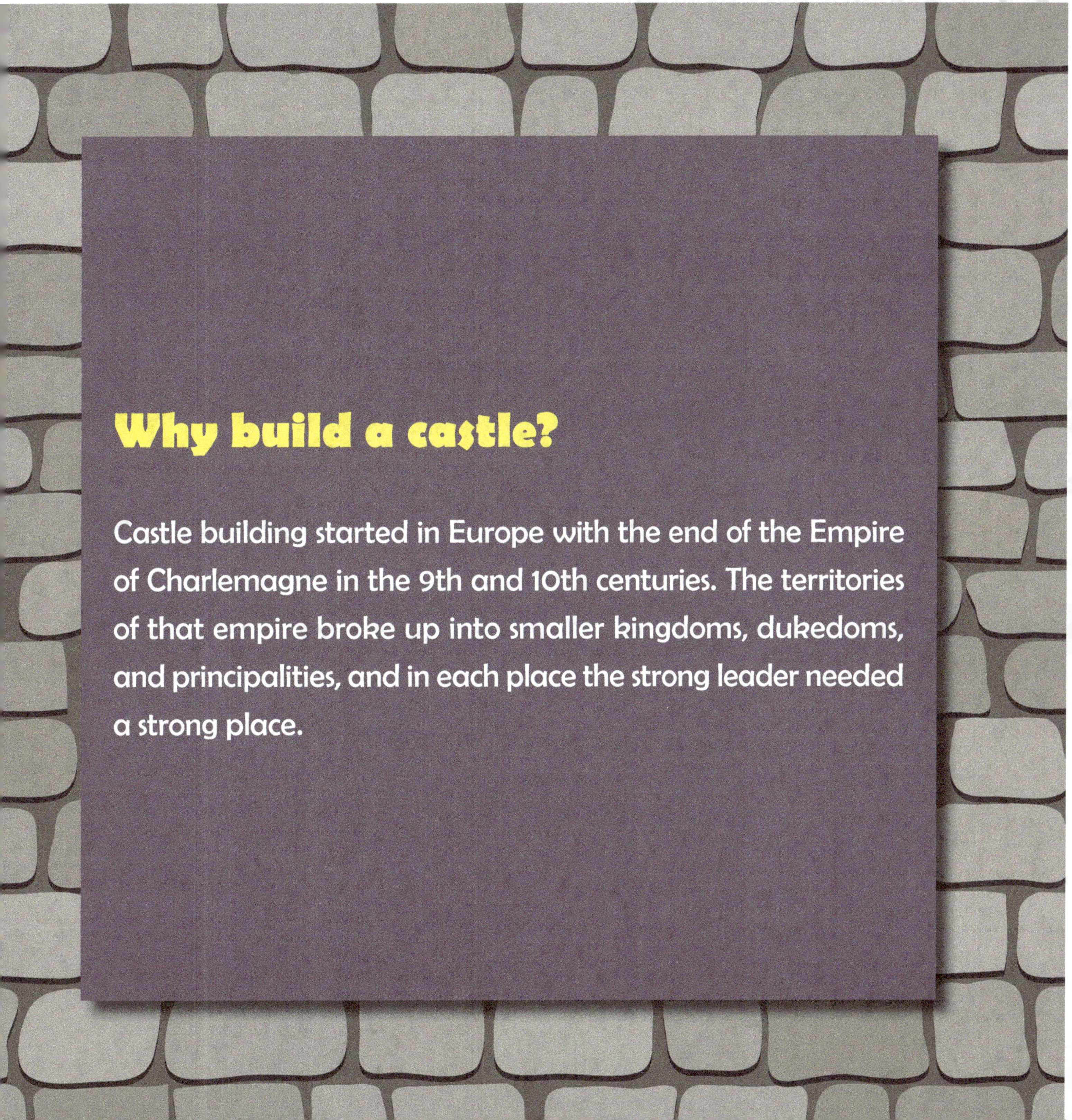

Why build a castle?

Castle building started in Europe with the end of the Empire of Charlemagne in the 9th and 10th centuries. The territories of that empire broke up into smaller kingdoms, dukedoms, and principalities, and in each place the strong leader needed a strong place.

The leader needed a strong place for several reasons. He wanted to show off his power and impress both his people and the leaders of other kingdoms who might otherwise be tempted to attack his territory. He needed a place to gather, train, and equip his forces before marching them out to attack an enemy. And he needed strong places which would help hold off an enemy who decided to invade his lands.

Historic city of Salzburg in Austria

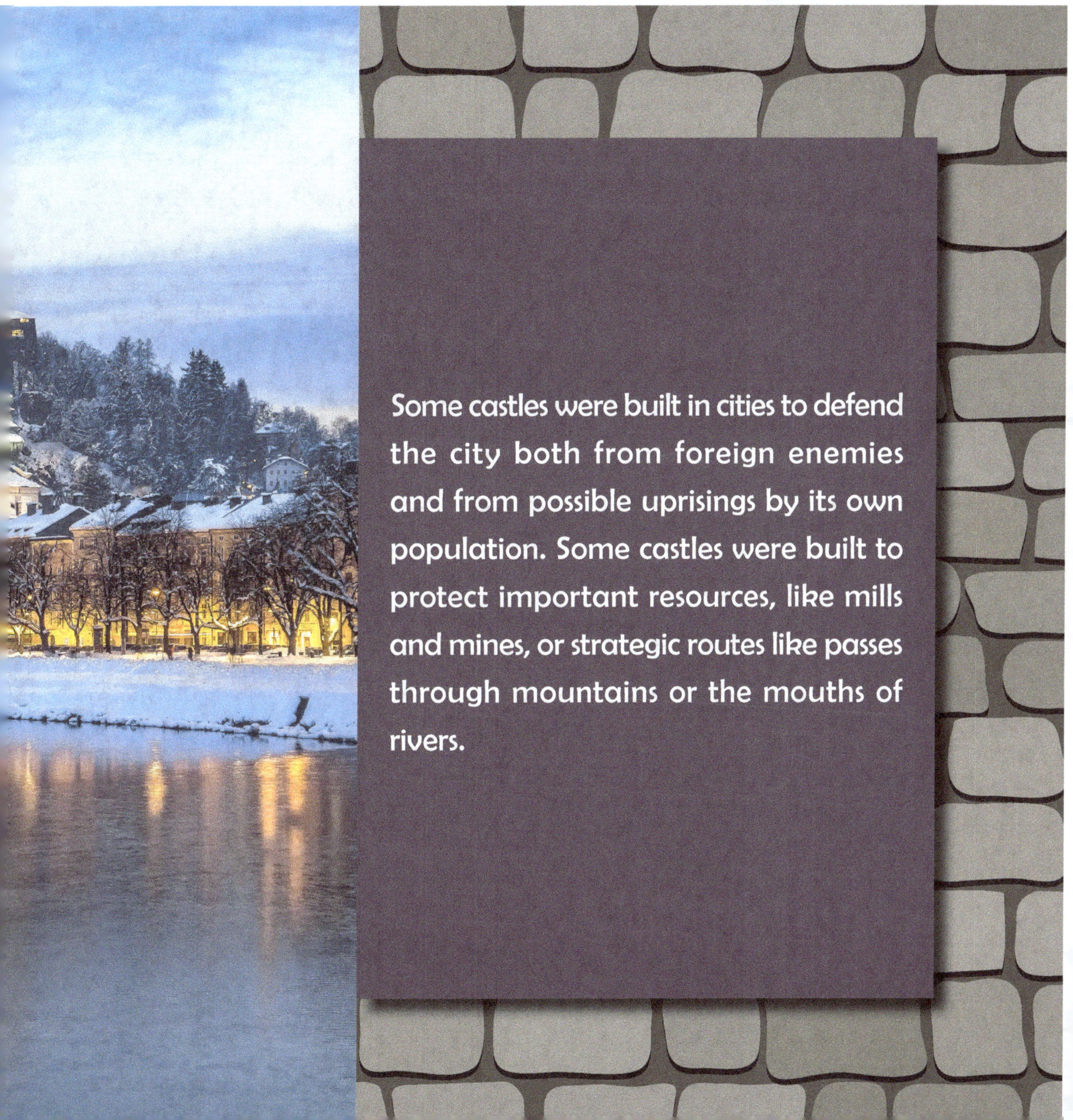

Some castles were built in cities to defend the city both from foreign enemies and from possible uprisings by its own population. Some castles were built to protect important resources, like mills and mines, or strategic routes like passes through mountains or the mouths of rivers.

A land could come under attack from within, as well as from other countries. After William the Conqueror invaded England and became its king in 1066, he faced a land that was largely hostile to him. Between 1066 and 1087 he established 36 castles throughout his lands. Most of these were designed to keep down the local people, not to defend against external threats.

William the Conqueror

Tower of London
"ENTRY TO THE TRAITORS' GATE

Castles also served as administrative centers, treasure-houses, and places to hold important prisoners. The Tower of London is a strong castle that was also a prison, and is still home to some of the greatest treasures of the UK government and the British monarchy, like the crown jewels.

In the fifteenth and sixteenth centuries the arrival of cannons and then artillery meant that castles started to change from being strong points to targets, and the age of castle-building came to an end. However, castles could still be pressed into use in emergencies. During World War II, the British military built a whole hidden complex of tunnels, control centers, weapons depots, and places for troops under Dover Castle, just across the English Channel from German-occupied France.

Cannons

Neuschwanstein Castle

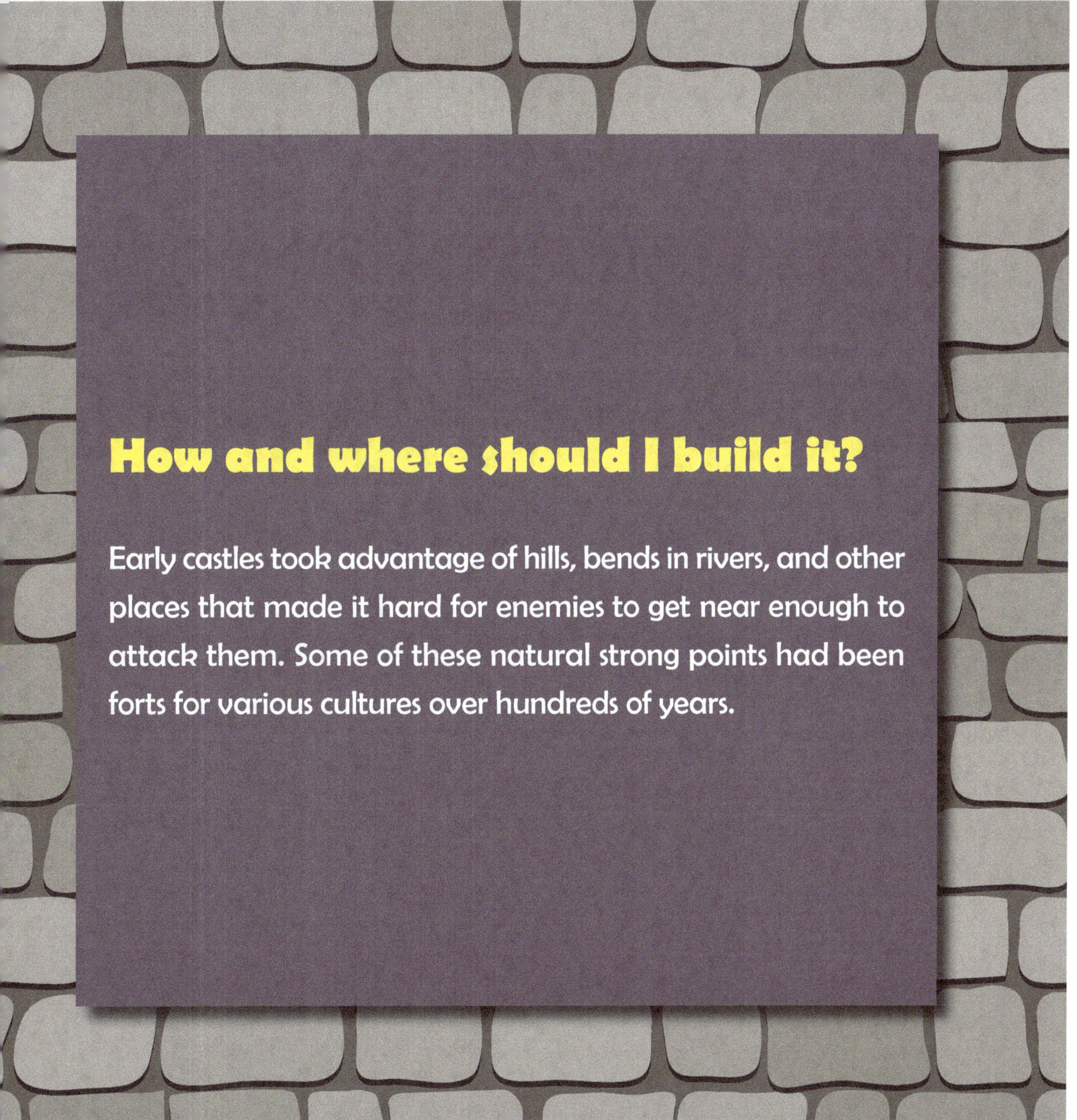

How and where should I build it?

Early castles took advantage of hills, bends in rivers, and other places that made it hard for enemies to get near enough to attack them. Some of these natural strong points had been forts for various cultures over hundreds of years.

As the science of castle-building progressed, it became less important to find a hill to put your castle on, and more important to put it where you needed it. The more modern castle, with many towers and a complex design so that other parts of the castle could support a part that came under attack, became its own mountain.

Caernarfon Castle

Here's the thing about building a castle, though: you'll need a lot of money and people to put it together. You want it to be so strong that an enemy would think twice before deciding to attack it. It needs to have space to hold your soldiers, space to hold horses for your cavalry, a way for them to defend the walls, and a way from them to quickly march out to attack the enemy. It was like building a brand new, well-defended city.

Parts of a castle

Not every castle has all the elements listed here, but these are standard parts of European castles.

Oyster bay Mansions

Motte

A motte is an earth, or earth and rock, mound with a flat top. The name is related to the word "moat" for a ditch, and for early strong points you could remove earth from what would become your moat and use it to build up your motte in the middle of the moat. The top edge of the motte would have at least a wooden palisade, if not a stone wall. The bailey would sit on top of the motte.

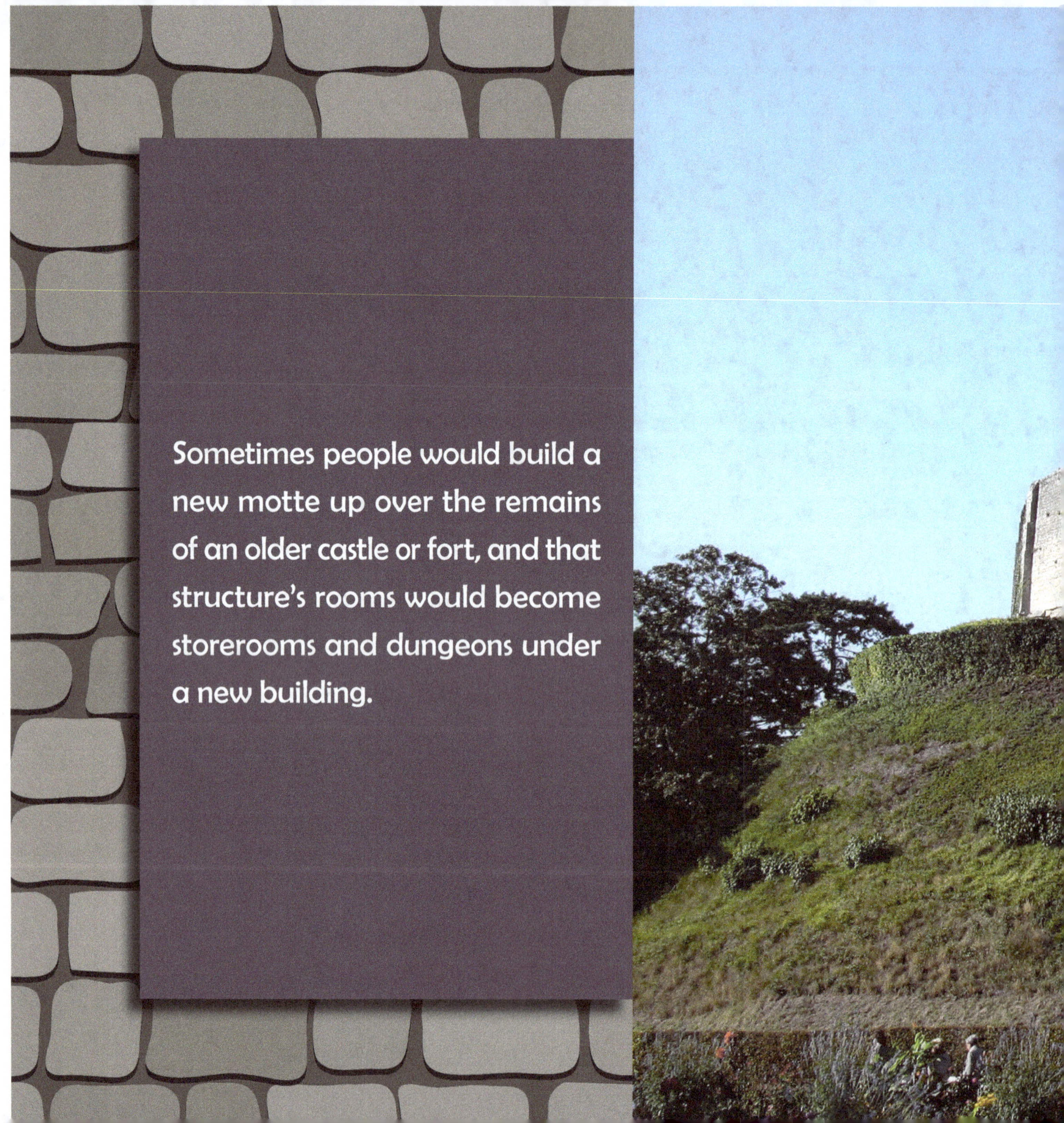

Sometimes people would build a new motte up over the remains of an older castle or fort, and that structure's rooms would become storerooms and dungeons under a new building.

Motte and Bailey Castle

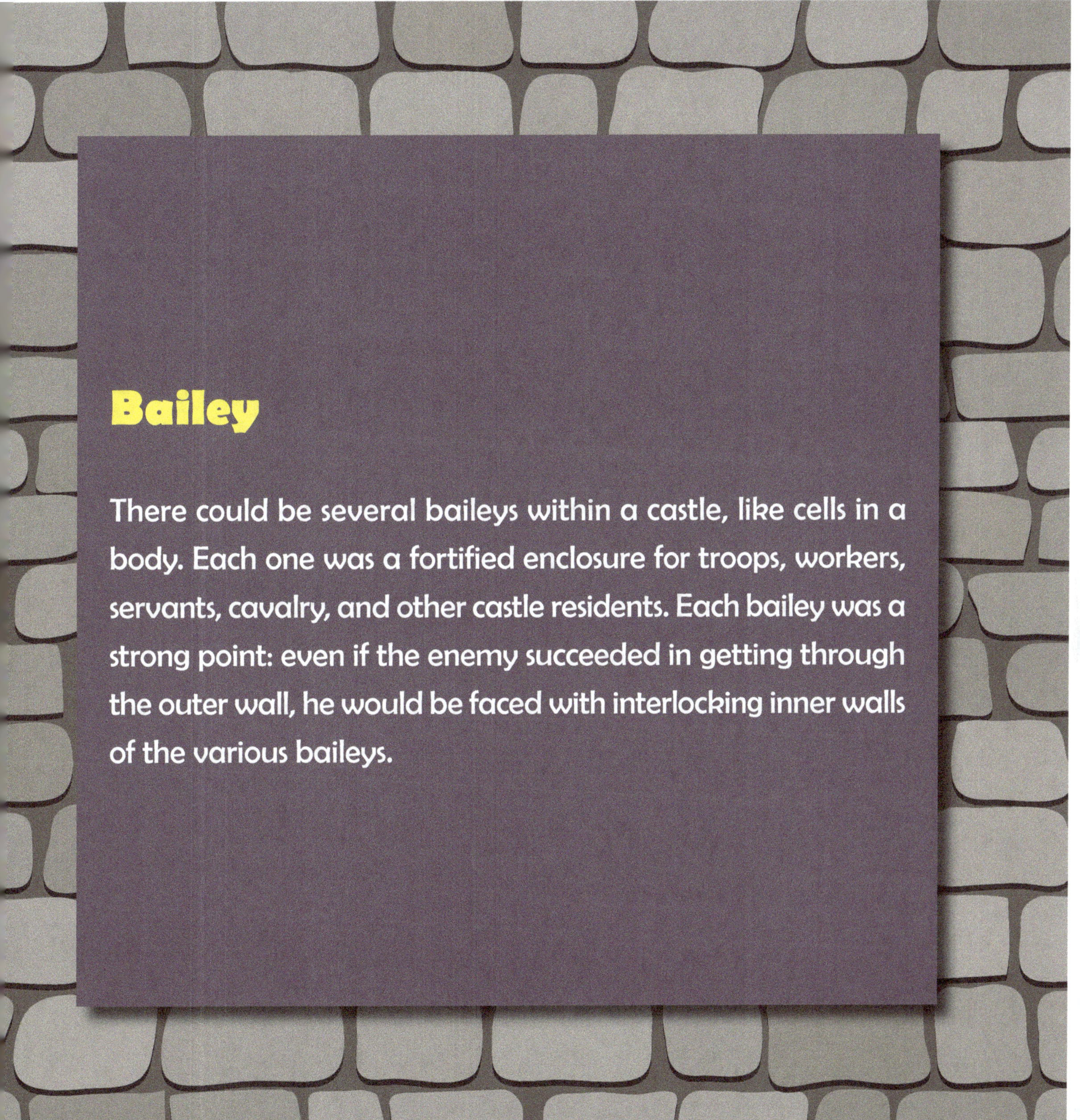

Bailey

There could be several baileys within a castle, like cells in a body. Each one was a fortified enclosure for troops, workers, servants, cavalry, and other castle residents. Each bailey was a strong point: even if the enemy succeeded in getting through the outer wall, he would be faced with interlocking inner walls of the various baileys.

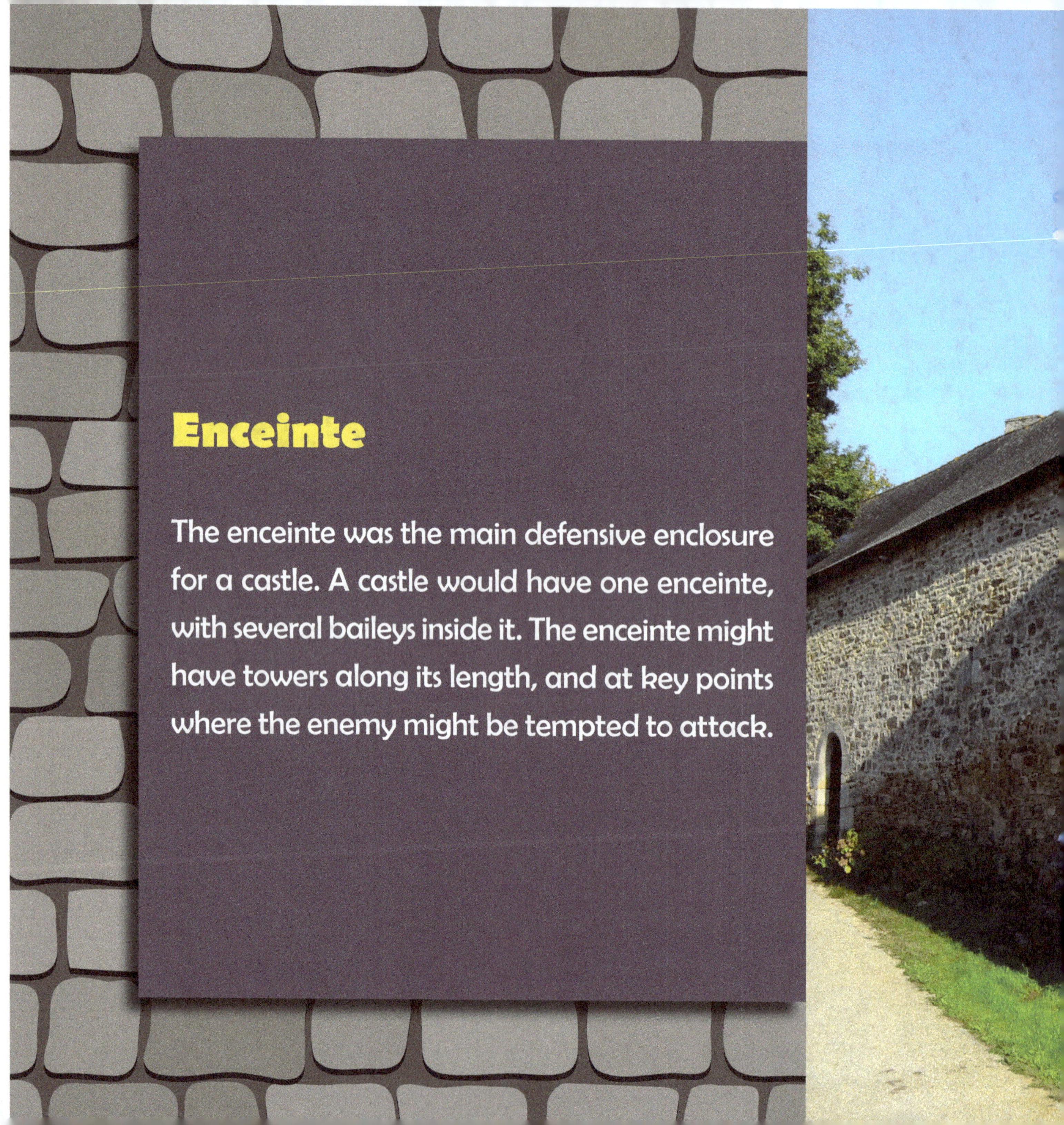

Enceinte

The enceinte was the main defensive enclosure for a castle. A castle would have one enceinte, with several baileys inside it. The enceinte might have towers along its length, and at key points where the enemy might be tempted to attack.

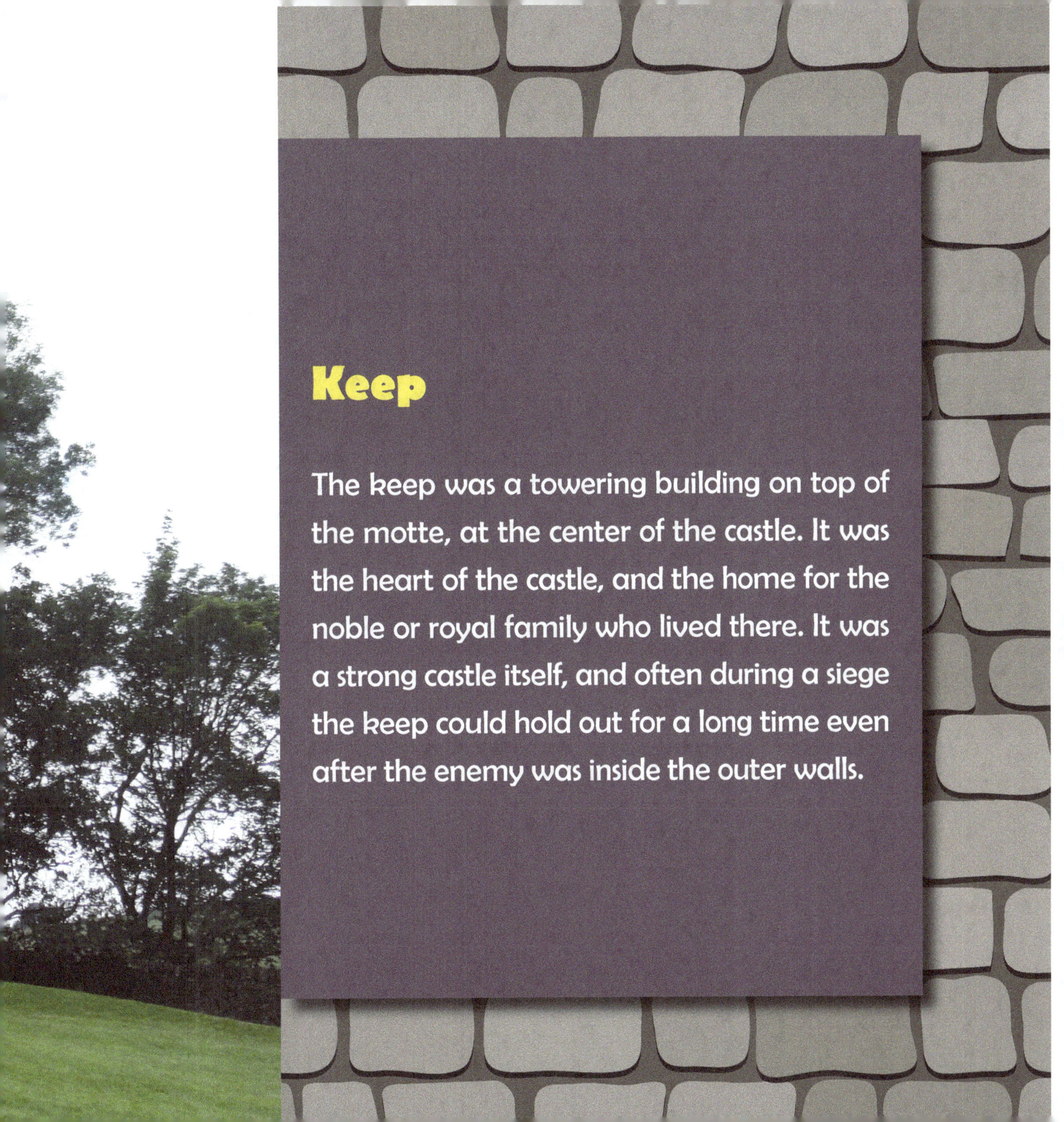

Keep

The keep was a towering building on top of the motte, at the center of the castle. It was the heart of the castle, and the home for the noble or royal family who lived there. It was a strong castle itself, and often during a siege the keep could hold out for a long time even after the enemy was inside the outer walls.

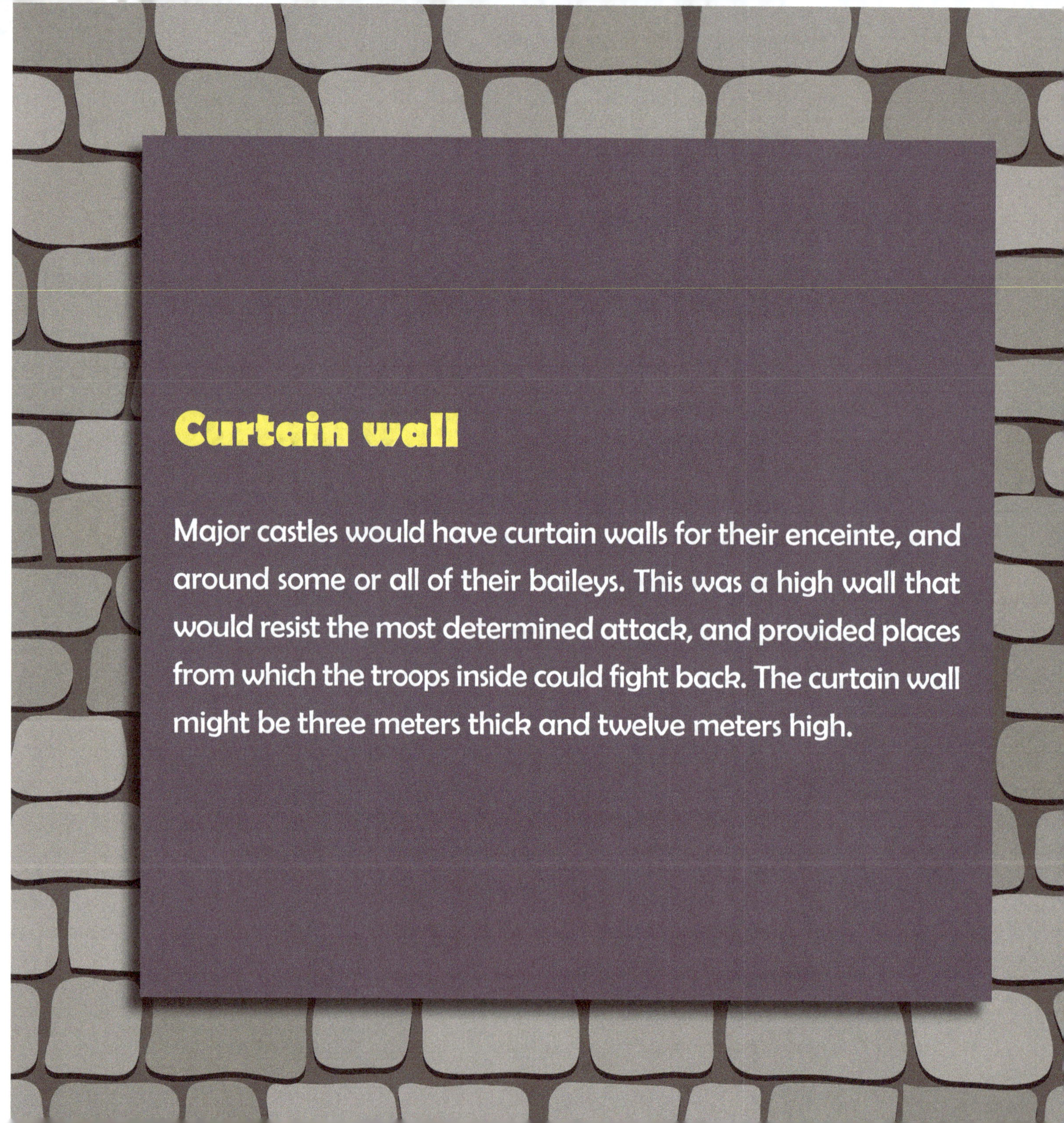

Curtain wall

Major castles would have curtain walls for their enceinte, and around some or all of their baileys. This was a high wall that would resist the most determined attack, and provided places from which the troops inside could fight back. The curtain wall might be three meters thick and twelve meters high.

Skipton Castle

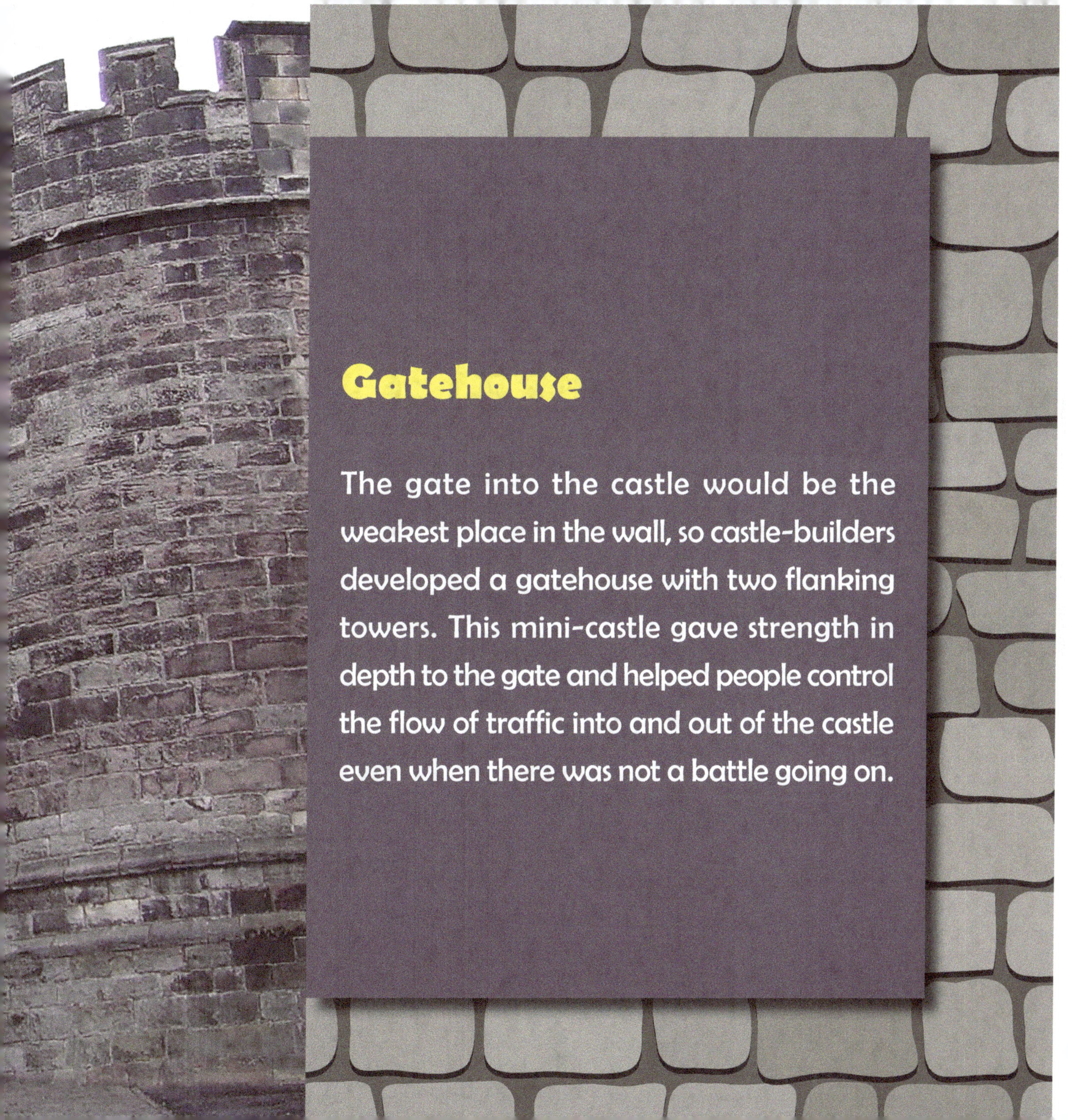

Gatehouse

The gate into the castle would be the weakest place in the wall, so castle-builders developed a gatehouse with two flanking towers. This mini-castle gave strength in depth to the gate and helped people control the flow of traffic into and out of the castle even when there was not a battle going on.

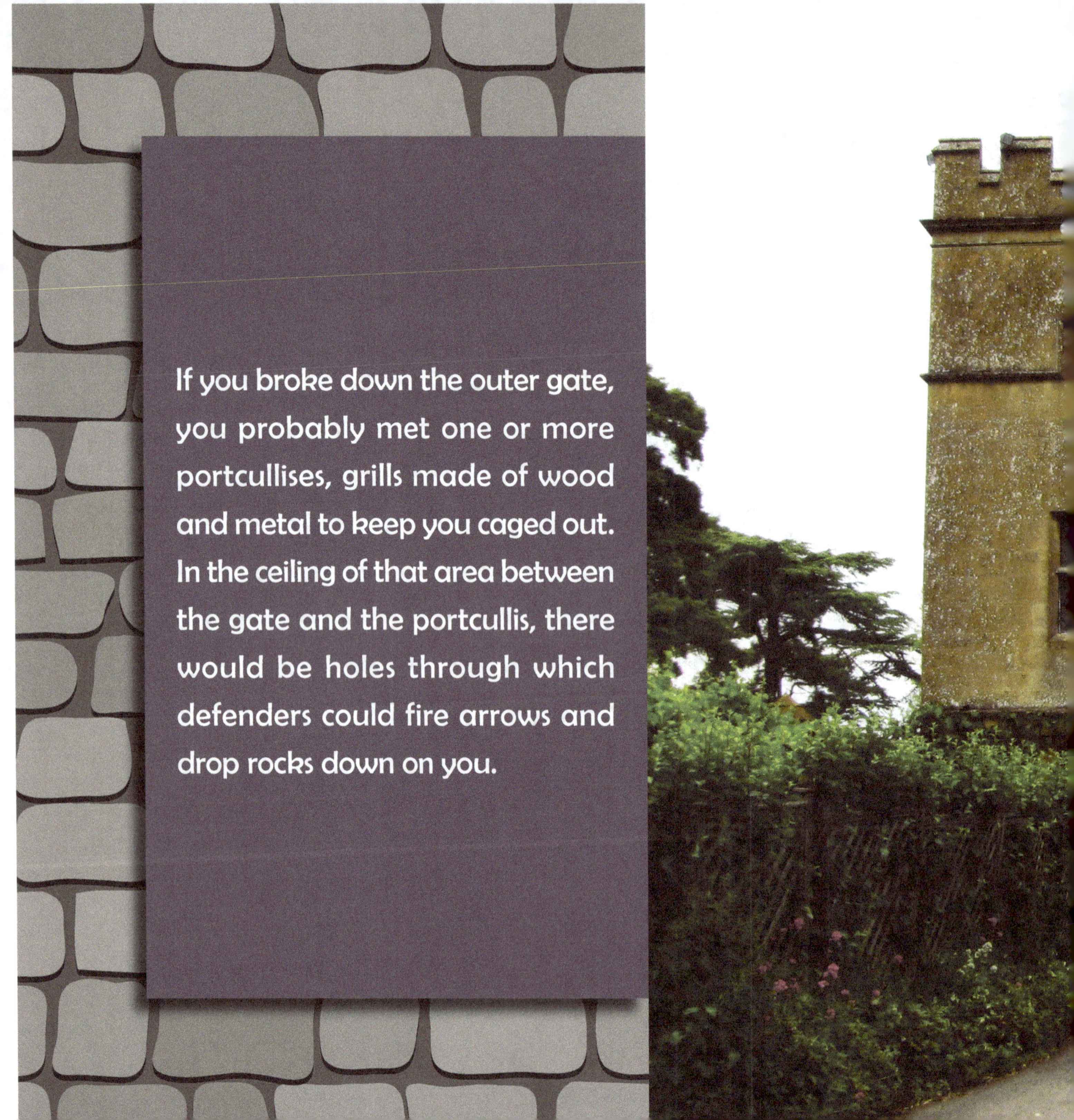
If you broke down the outer gate, you probably met one or more portcullises, grills made of wood and metal to keep you caged out. In the ceiling of that area between the gate and the portcullis, there would be holes through which defenders could fire arrows and drop rocks down on you.

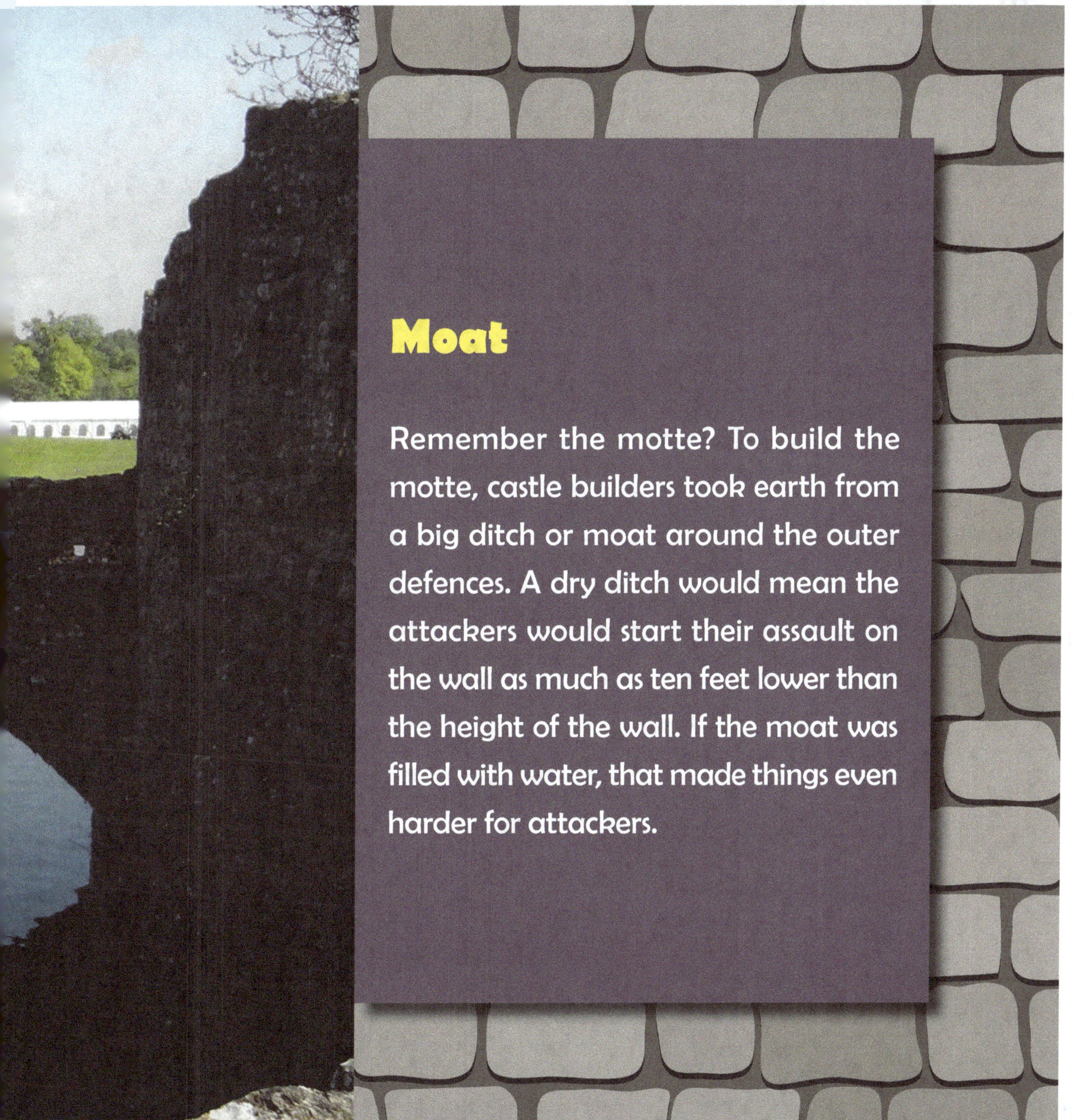

Moat

Remember the motte? To build the motte, castle builders took earth from a big ditch or moat around the outer defences. A dry ditch would mean the attackers would start their assault on the wall as much as ten feet lower than the height of the wall. If the moat was filled with water, that made things even harder for attackers.

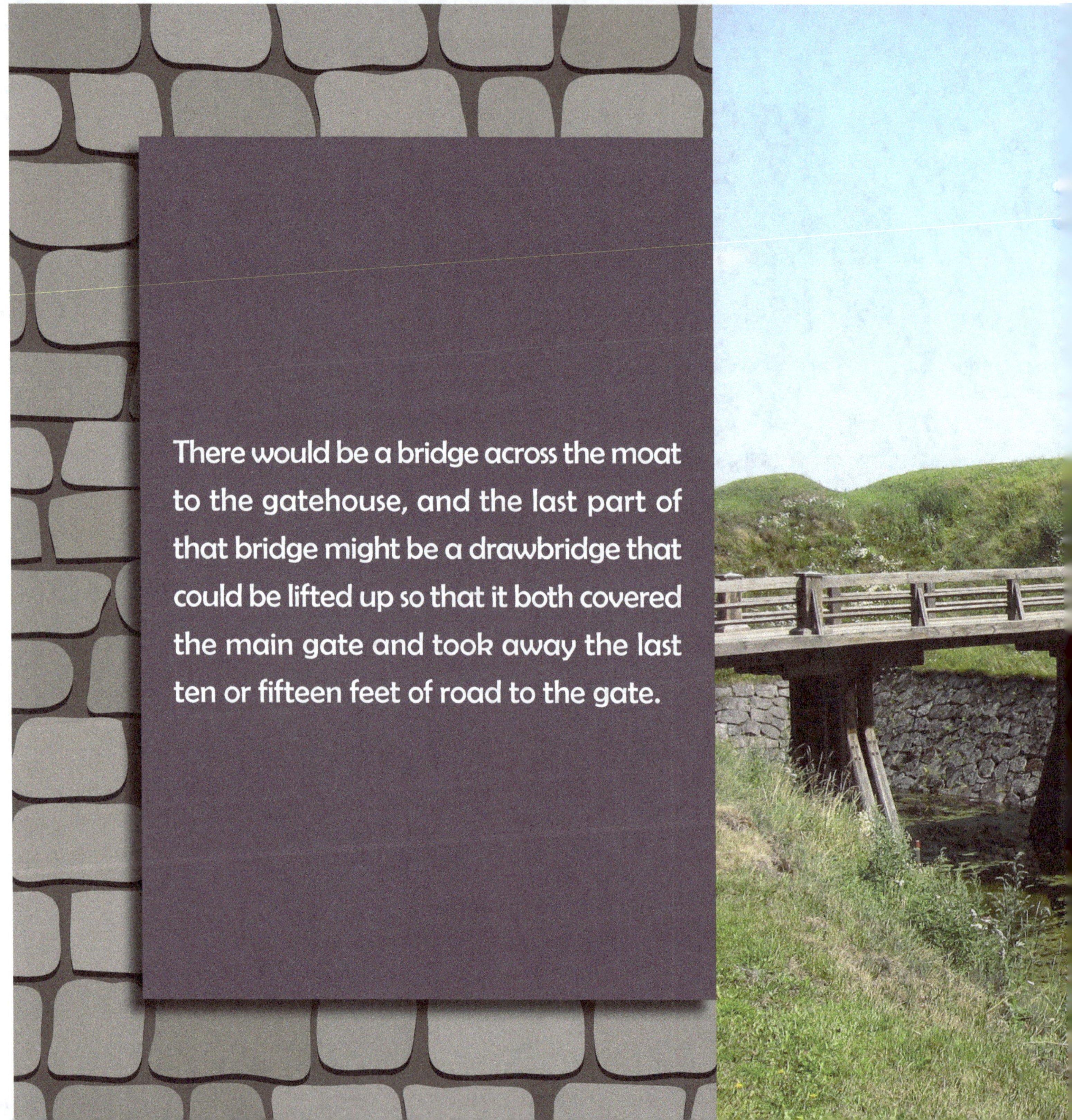

There would be a bridge across the moat to the gatehouse, and the last part of that bridge might be a drawbridge that could be lifted up so that it both covered the main gate and took away the last ten or fifteen feet of road to the gate.

Battlements

Battlements on top of the curtain walls were in part a fringe of stone blocks which helped protectors as they fired down on attackers. There were also wooden and stone structures that extended out beyond the walls, so defenders could send arrows and stones straight down at the attacking army as it drew close to the wall, without exposing themselves by leaning out over the wall.

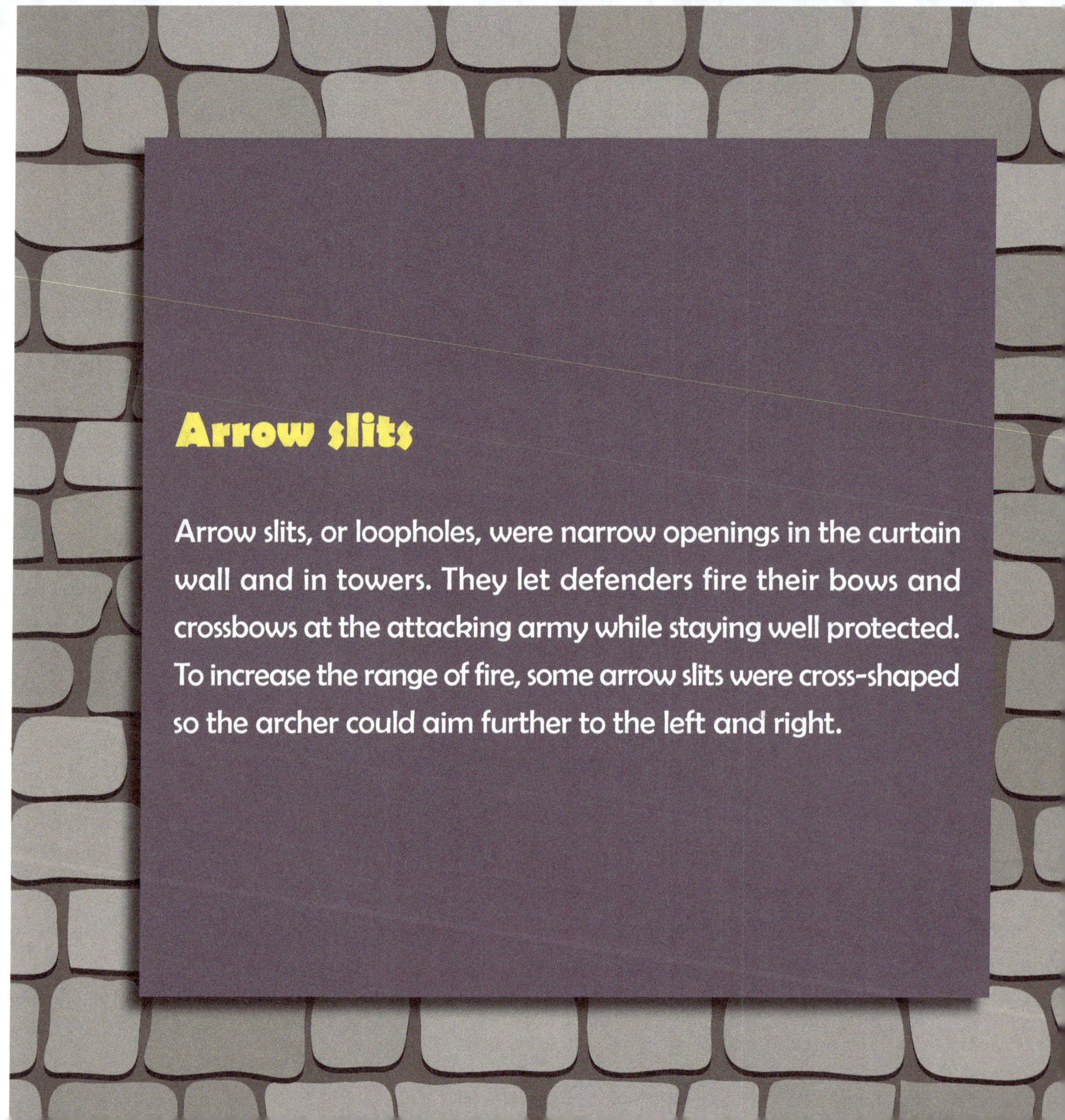

Arrow slits

Arrow slits, or loopholes, were narrow openings in the curtain wall and in towers. They let defenders fire their bows and crossbows at the attacking army while staying well protected. To increase the range of fire, some arrow slits were cross-shaped so the archer could aim further to the left and right.

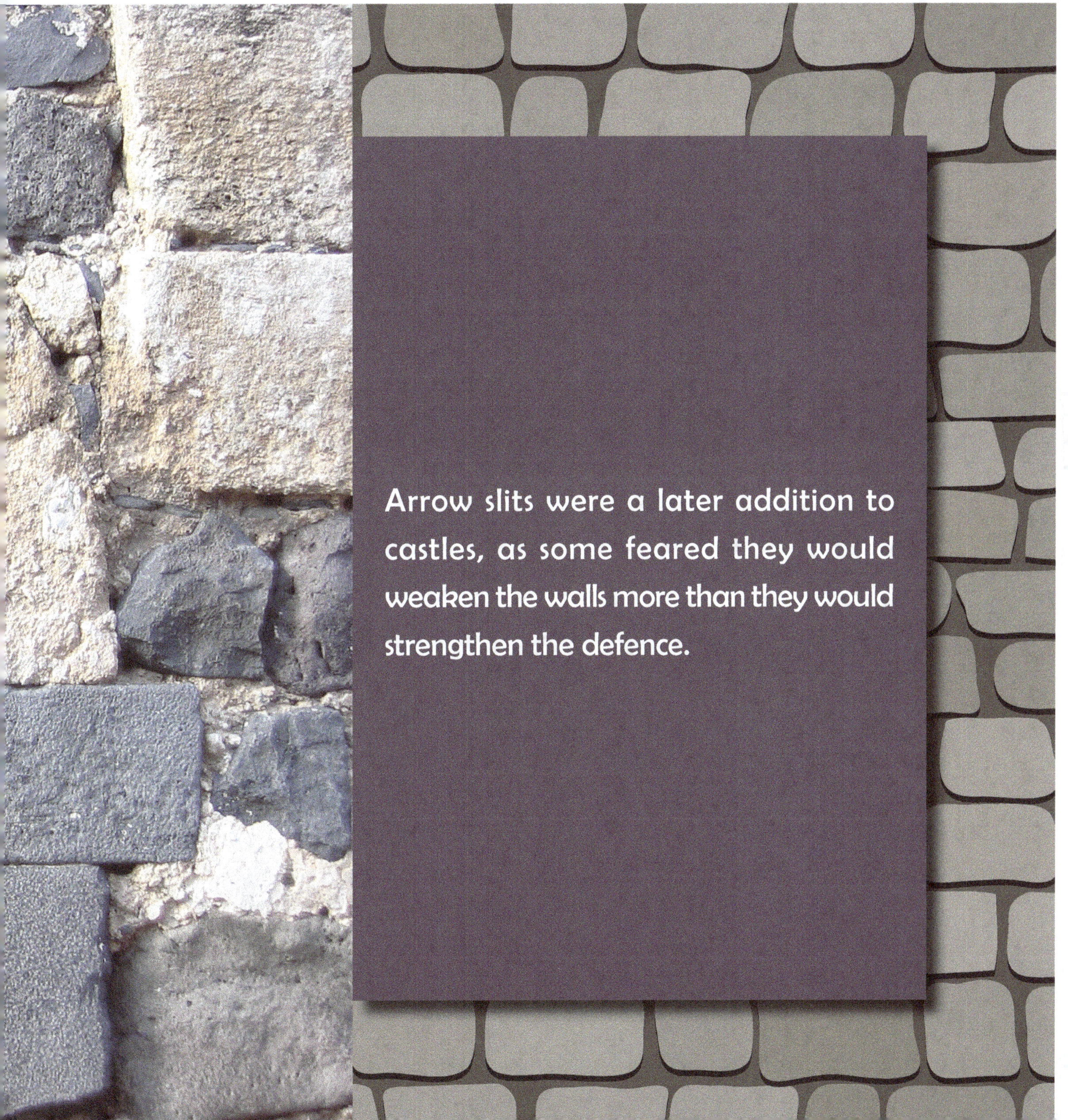
Arrow slits were a later addition to castles, as some feared they would weaken the walls more than they would strengthen the defence.

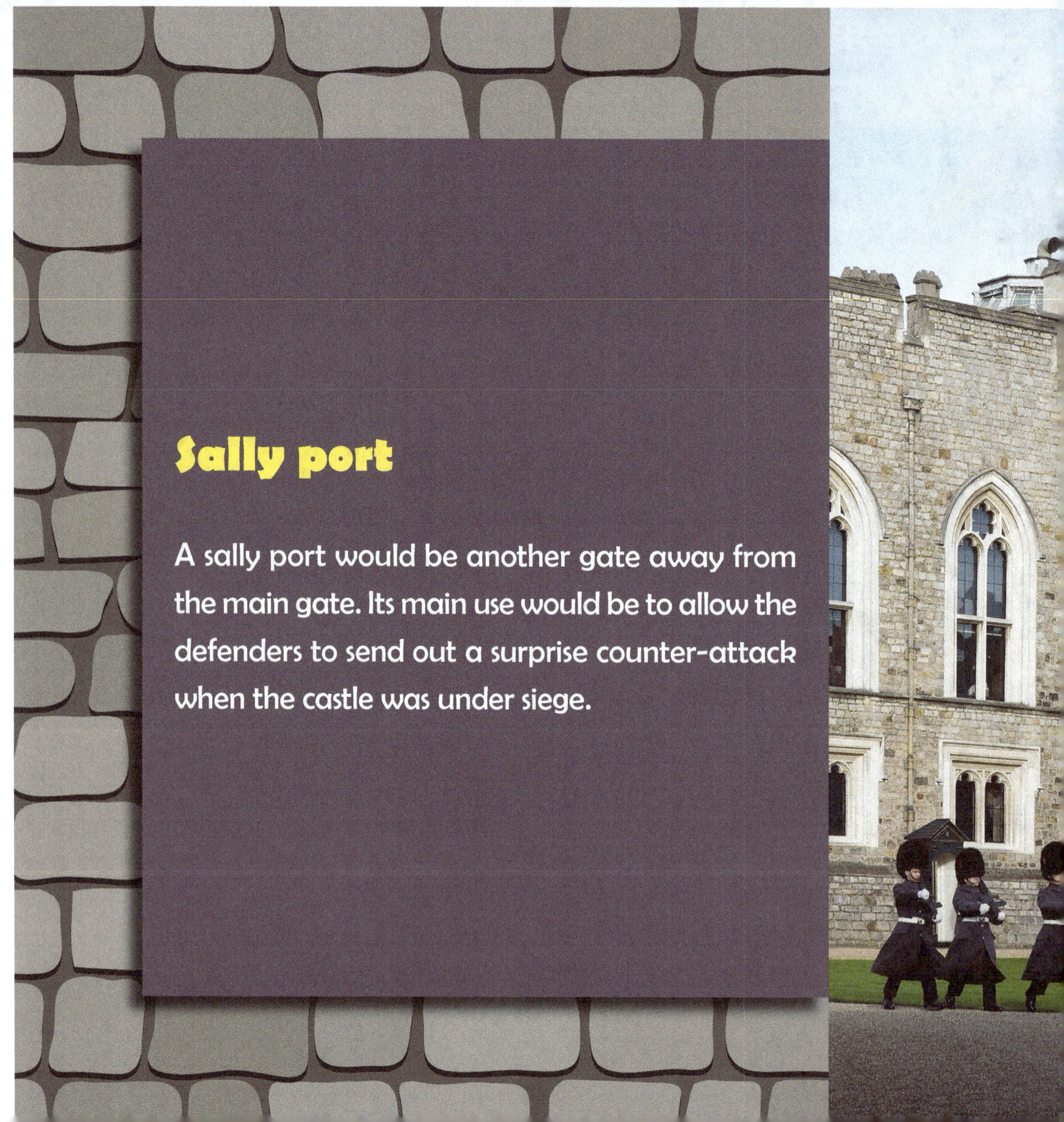

Sally port

A sally port would be another gate away from the main gate. Its main use would be to allow the defenders to send out a surprise counter-attack when the castle was under siege.

St George's Chapel, Windsor Castle

More than pretty buildings

There is a lot more to learn about the time when people lived in castles. Read Baby Professor books like How to Become a Knight and Daily Struggles of Those who Lived in the Middle Ages to learn more!

Gothic Castle

Visit
BABY PROFESSOR
EDUCATION KIDS
www.BabyProfessorBooks.com
to download Free Baby Professor eBooks
and view our catalog of new and exciting
Children's Books

www.ingramcontent.com/pod-product-compliance
Lightning Source LLC
Chambersburg PA
CBHW081057140726
48009CB00014B/199